50+1
Horror Movies

FABIO CONSIGLIO

DEDICATION

I would like to dedicate this book to all monsters, zombies, ghosts, vampires, demons and fictional killers that inspire me and are much less frightening than the real human beings.

CONTENTS

Introduction   i

1   Demons   3

2   Splatter   17

3   Ghosts   24

4   Vampires   49

5   Monsters   57

6   Zombies   65

7   Miscellaneous   75

8   Anthologies   95

9   +1 Horror Movie   104

INTRODUCTION

This book brings together a selection of 50 texts about horror movies written in 2017 on the Portuguese language blog http://faroartesepsicologia.blogspot.com.br. There are some short and longer texts, not necessarily proportional to the quality of the film but what the movie has done for me - all criticism reveals more of its author than of the analyzed object.

The title 50+1 Horror Movies: 50 texts by me and an invited author, the Visual Arts Master and Education, Art and History of Culture Ph.D. Rosângela Donizete Canassa, who wrote about Perfume: The Story of a Murderer.

Fabio Consiglio

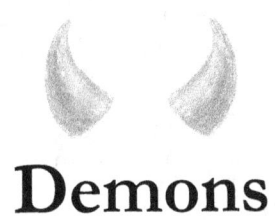

Demons

Rosemary's Baby (1968)

There are no scares, monsters or blood, and yet *Rosemary's Baby* is scary. Using only the cinematographic art to create suggestion - many people swear they have seen the baby and how he or she looks horrible, even with the child never being shown in the movie - Roman Polanski created a masterpiece of supernatural terror or a drama about an extremely disturbed pregnant woman, it is up to those who watch to decide.

Rosemary (Mia Farrow) and Guy Woodhouse (John Cassavetes) move to a new apartment, surrounded by strange neighbors who come to meddle in the life of the couple. Initially reluctant about this new friendship, Guy suddenly join the neighbors' residence and encourages Rosemary to bond, until the girl becomes pregnant and things get more and more unusual.

There is a great deal of care with the details in *Rosemary's Baby* and everything that appears on the screen is relevant at some point in a clue-reward game that gives pleasure to the audience: the fear of touching Rosemary's belly demonstrated by Guy, the neighbor Roman Castevet (Sidney Blackmer) who at the New Year party announces that that will be year number one, the Woodhouse couple playing scrabble, game that will be important to unravel part of the plot. All these clues are spread naturally and fluently, never seeming to have been planted just to generate astonishment in the public. Another right decision is the composition of the character Rosemary, that demonstrates be innocent and passive like a child and her personality allows us to believe she is able to do things by following other people's commands

It is possible consider the whole story of *Rosemary's Baby* as a set of coincidences and hallucinations and the director himself Roman Polanski claims to have left everything ambiguous in a purposeful way. I cannot see it that way, because although there is some ambiguity the number of coincidences is so great when we discount the supernatural element that is easier to embrace the most obvious and fantastic explanation: Rosemary's baby really is the son of the devil. But that does not matter, what does not come out of the head at the end of *Rosemary's Baby* is when someone says "He has his father's eyes" without the baby being shown, letting each viewer imagine the baby's appearance; nothing better to create the darkest nightmares than our own imagination.

Score: 5/5

The Exorcist (1973)

To this day, more than 40 years later, *The Exorcist* is still scary and not only because of the extremely convincing scenes of Regan's (Linda Blair) possession, but for all the atmosphere created in its first half that makes, like the priest Karras (Jason Miller), we were even frightened with the telephone's ring.

There are other things to notice in *The Exorcist* besides the well-constructed horror scenes. The characters have been developed so that each one has its own devil: Father Karras with the loss of his faith and guilt for the abandonment and death of his mother, Chris (Ellen Burstyn) with his divorce and the troubled relationship with the ex-husband and father of Regan, the exorcist Merrin (Max von Sydow) with the death lurking by the chronic illness. The Regan girl, pure and yet without her own fears to be haunted, was the perfect victim of the devil and the fact of possession being in a child potentiates the terror and shock caused by *The Exorcist*.

To further intensify fear, several images of demons are displayed quickly, almost subliminally. When we watch in the home video, the tendency is to go back to the scene and check what we think we have seen; I can imagine the effect of this on theater, where it would be impossible to have absolute certainty of what was exhibited, increasing the discomfort in order to make the whole experience more powerful.

The Exorcist has aged very well even in the special effects issues and makeup, which remain convincing even in the digital era. Its cadenced rhythm, far from causing monotony, keep increasing the discomfort and dread in the audience preparing the apotheosis of the exorcism of the final sprint. Even to the unbelievers, who see god and the devil as mythological figures, to watch *The Exorcist* at night and alone is a challenge.

Score: 4/5

Hellraiser (1987)

Hellraiser can be seen as a metaphor for the dangers of hedonism or even related to the recent (in 1987) AIDS epidemic. Whether or not these meanings are viewed, *Hellraiser* is a good horror movie that avoids easy frights by investing in development of the characters, using their monsters as the embodiment of the darkest desires of men.

Looking for extreme sadomasochistic pleasures, Frank (Sean Chapman) invokes the so-called cenobite demons to help him by using a puzzle box that once solved conjures up the creatures. He dies during the experience but his essence survives somehow until the day that his former lover Julia (Clare Higgins), the wife of Frank's brother, accidentally resurrects him.

What makes *Hellraiser* interesting is the doubt about which we should fear the most, the cenobites or Frank and Julia? The really scary element is the supernatural or the flesh and blood real people? The cenobites are only a reflection of the sadism present in the people, from the innocent morbid curiosity of those who interrupt their journey in order to see a victim of an accident, even the torturers who come to feel sexual pleasure by inflicting torments on their victims.

The completion of the film closes the conjuring box cycle in Frank's hands, restarting the cube's journey. The conclusion, although it seems to have been made with the purpose of generating continuations, makes all sense: interested in the puzzles and the pleasures offered by the cenobites will never miss, as there will always be people attracted by the satisfaction that suffering - own or the other ones - can provide.

Score: 3/5

The Unborn (2009)

What distinguishes *The Unborn* from so many other films dealing with possessive spirits is the folklore behind the plot, here not the Christian-Catholic but the Hebrew. But this "innovation" does not save the film of mediocrity.

Casey (Odette Annable) is being pursued by a dybbuk (possessing spirit of Jewish folklore) and seeks to find out the reasons and how to escape from the entity. Nothing in the plot makes much sense, beginning with the spirit's motivation, involving the connection between twins and the past of Casey's family in the Auschwitz Concentration Camp (until the Nazi Josef Mengele is quoted), up to the methods of the entity, which uses tortuous ways to realize possession - the final revelation further weakens the story.

Like every mediocre horror movie, *The Unborn* fulfills exhibition time with irrelevant frights to the plot, using dreams and hallucinations, everything to convince the viewer that something is happening when in fact nothing is actually taking the story forward.

There is a hidden meaning in *The Unborn* related to terrorism, conveying the message that acts of terror (the real ones, not those of the spirits) are not associated with a specific religion; this can be observed by phrases such as "we are not safe anywhere", "can be any of us" and by the exorcism ritual showing ecumenical character, joining Jews and Christians. If metaphorically the message of the film were a gift, we can say that it is so small and so poorly packed that it is not worth the effort to unwrap it.

Score: 2/5

Satanic (2016)

Four futile and not very busy young people head to Los Angeles for dark sightseeing - staying in a suicide hotel room, visiting the house where Sharon Tate's assassination took place by Charles Manson's followers, and shopping in satanic shops. Obviously our heroes find more than they seek and end up engaging in a supernatural story involving demon worshipers.

There is only one good thing about *Satanic*, its rhythm; but if on the one hand the film is not boring, on the other hand everything happens quickly so that the audience does not have time to realize how bad the plot is and the interpretations are shallow - nothing like a dynamic editing to hide defects.

The attitudes of girls and boys, typical young Americans often portrayed by the cinema as stupid and ignorant, are inexplicable and incoherent, not allowing the creation of an immersive story since their attitudes are strictly artificial. There's still a temporal loop without meaning and without consequences - I think about the meeting of the filmmakers and producers imagining the movie and making the decision: let's put something related to the time in our film, it will be cool and look smart!

In a way *Satanic* makes the life of the audience easy: to choose who deserves our support in the supernatural journey, since with so despicable characters it is very easy to wish that the devil quickly completes its mission to take all of them to hell.

Score: 2/5

Under the Shadow (2016)

A family is persecuted by djinn (supernatural creature or demon mentioned in Islamic theology) in this Iranian terror that took place in the initial period of the Iran-Iraq War (1980-88).

Under the Shadow is a modest movie with great performances and the entity - the djinn – fortunately avoid the Hollywood demons' stereotypes. Making a clear analogy of the djinn's arrival with the social restrictions imposed by the recently implanted Islamic Revolution, *Under the Shadow* is not limited to supernatural terror; the most frightening is the social and religious horror.

Score: 4/5

It (2017)

It is electrifying as a ghost train ride, where every fright gives satisfaction and generates relief after the tension is over. Behind an extremely well made and entertaining work, one can see elements far more frightening than Pennywise Clown.

Little Derry, Maine, holds a terrifying secret behind its abnormally high numbers of disappearances: the city is home to a clown-shape creature that captures and devours people, especially children, in the form of the most obscure fears stored in their victims' minds. Based on Stephen King's homonymous book, *It* manages to transpose onto the screen the atmosphere of the fear and bond from the children that face Pennywise (Bill Skarsgård), adapting and updating the first part of the story, with the characters still pre-adolescents (the book was in 1959, the film in 1989). There are beautiful scenes, such as early in the story of the boy running behind the paper boat using bird's eye shot, and the scary ones, the clown coming out of the screen during a slide projection and attacking the children - this is especially interesting by the metalanguage involved, since makes us fear if Pennywise would not leave the movie screen to devour us.

But the real dread caused by *It* does not come from the monster, but from the people, and Pennywise only reflects the cruelty in each of them, including children. What about a bullie that torments younger children to the point of writing their own name with a pocketknife on the victim's skin? Or the father who sexually insinuates himself to his daughter, almost to the point of abusing her?

In addition we have the main meaning that hides in the legend of the devouring monster, insinuated by the cycle of Pennywise, which appears of 27 in 27 years, very close to the time that is usually defined as a generation, 25 years. In the film we see that children are ignored, created negligently, as if they were unwanted. Pennywise, with the connivance of adults, would then be responsible for eliminating inconvenient offspring, performing a late abortion, abortion that was not done in the gestational period because of religious, family, or lack of courage. Is Pennywise a treacherous demon or just an executioner of the honest people's unconfessable desires?

Score: 4/5

Splatter

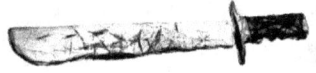

At Midnight I'll Take Your Soul (1964)

José Mojica Marins is a pioneer of Brazilian horror movies and still today he is its most known artist. In *At Midnight I'll Take Your* Soul Mojica introduce us the gravedigger Coffin Joe, the main character and filmmaker's cinematographic persona.

The great merit of *At Midnight I'll Take Your Soul* is to create a genuinely Brazilian terror, not trying to imitate the Hollywood horror sthetics. It is heavily based in Catholic traditions, such as holy days and processions, but also features elements such as santeria, reflecting the strong Brazilian religious syncretism.

In this broth of belief, the greatest sin is to be a non-believing, in the movie and in real life; the atheist, the one who has no god in his heart, is the supreme villain - Coffin Joe is like that - and the film shows this clearly. It is painful to realize that even today this idea reigns - every atheist has noticed some kind of prejudice.

With a modest but efficient production - even the makeup effects work very well - *At Midnight* fulfills its goals of scaring and has the bonus of making us think how much this religiosity of the Brazilian people is really healthy. Perhaps this blind belief could explain the Coffin Joe international success and his lack of recognition in Brazil.

Score: 4/5

Friday the 13th (1980)

Chi chi chi chi chi... Cha cha cha cha cha... Ahhh, the good old Jason theme before he thread his machete into some teenager having sex or smoking a joint. But before the *Friday the 13th* movies franchise became a ridiculous formula for boys grab their girlfriends at the movies, the first *Friday*, far from being a great movie at least it was decent. Less bloody and not risible like its sequels, we see here some interesting ideas and the good makeup of Tom Savini. Watch and then ask your friends: How many people did Jason kill on the original *Friday the 13th*? The answer, for anyone who has not seen the movie, will be surprising.

Score: 3/5

My Soul to Take (2010)

Wes Craven has created very successful horror franchises: *A Nightmare on Elm Street*, introducing Freddy Krueger who is now an important part of pop culture and *Scream*, that innovated playing around with the conventions of the teen horror genre. But *My Soul to Take* is lackluster, it sound like just recycling ideas with no personality.

The old and beaten murderer returning plot, coming back to take revenge and kill everyone for any reason, this is the *My Soul to Take* full storyline. It's all generic, from the double personality of the original murderer to the old litany of the American school with its fauna - the nerds, the bullies, the preppie girls. It's hard to handle the first two-thirds of the movie, which improves somewhat with the turnaround of the third act, but at this point the audience (and patience) are already lost.

It seems that with *My Soul to Take* Wes Craven tried once again to create a movie franchise, since the structure of the film and the way the killer "works" had allowed endless continuations, but the lack of charisma and the production doing things automatically led to failure.

Score: 2/5

Grave (2016)

Grave (also known as *Raw*) is a Franco-Belgian drama with elements of horror that sins by its irregularity, but which if seen as metaphor gains new contours.

There is a certain exaggeration in several moments of the story of Justine (Garance Marillier), a vegetarian who becomes a veterinary student and is taken to try meat during the college trot, event from which the girl starts to feel an irresistible attraction for animal protein including that of human origin. The excesses are so much in the graphic aspect, with some scenes that exaggerate in violence and gore, as in the behavior of the characters, with Justine who seems not to be surprised with its behavioral changes. The film becomes more interesting and gains some depth if we associate Justine's trot and transformation with the rituals of initiation into adult life; Justine ceases to be vegetarian or innocent and sees the world as it really is, with each wanting to devour the other and therefore to overcome you must be the predator and not the prey.

Seeing *Grave* as a fable about the transition from childhood to adulthood, the film becomes something more than a mere distraction; if we do not take the metaphor into consideration, *Grave* is restricted to fans of a bloodthirsty and not subtle cinema.

Score: 3/5

FABIO CONSIGLIO

Ghosts

The Tomb of Ligeia (1964)

Directed by Roger Corman, the master of B movies, *The Tomb of Ligeia* presents the typical qualities and defects of this type of film: it has an excellent argument based on an Edgar Allan Poe short story, a few good ideas but also gives us moments which cause unintentional laughter.

Verden Fell (Vincent Price) is obsessed by his late wife Ligeia and sees the dead beloved in his current bride, Rowena Trevanion (Elizabeth Shepherd). From there the plot unfolds, casting doubt on whether Ligeia is really dead, about Verden sanity and if there would be any supernatural element involved. Verden's style, looking like a rock star, is a great hit. On the other hand, Price's interpretation is exaggerated and over-affected, which may even have been purposeful but helps to increase the fake feeling of the movie.

The film probably set a new record of pitching black cats in people, there being at least ten scenes in *The Tomb of Ligeia* in which this occurs. The lack of creativity in the film plans gets to bother after some time and the only feeling that these scenes provoke is affliction by the well-being of the feline. As already quoted, it is hard to avoid laughter when we see the cat jumping on someone's face for the third time in the last 5 minutes, everything being watched by a big ham Vincent Price.

The Tomb of Ligeia entertains, mainly by the force of its story, but the immersion becomes almost impossible in front of the problems pointed out, being in the middle of way between a horror movie and a comedy (although involuntary). Poe's work deserved a better stuff.

Score: 2/5

The Shining (1980)

There are movies that are so iconic and poweRful that they become part of the collective unconscious. *The Shining* is certainly one of those films.

In *The Shining* there are pictures that do not leave our minds: the tricycle strolling in the seemingly endless hotEl, the twins, the sea of blood, the labyrinth, all imitated and satirized to exhaustion, giving us the impression that the film is much older than it is.

Moreover, another thing that makes *The Shining* fascinating is its openness to many interpretations: what would be the cause of Jack's insanity? The loneliness and iDleness, Native American revenge, other lives settle accounts, or was he just always been that way and just had not had the opportunity to act? *The Shining* allows us to choose the answeR by showing us elements that justify any of them. There are even crazy theories that are in the *Room 237* documentary of 2012, bUt it takes a lot of goodwill to agree with them.

The Shining is perhaps the most perfect nightmare ever shot, a nightMare we do not want to wake up.

Score: 5/5

Beetlejuice (1988)

A couple of protagonists who dies early in the show and a bio-exorcist - an opposite exorcist, who expels the living: these things byself show the ability to subvert the expectations of the public and the creativity of *Beetlejuice*. The movie, most worried to surprise than to remain consistent, fails in the plot but has become part of pop culture with its characters and cartoon look.

Adam (Alec Baldwin) and Barbara Maitland (Geena Davis) love their home and they are constantly pressured to sell the house by broker Jane (Annie McEnroe). The couple dies in an accident and now, being ghosts, refuse to leave the home they loved so much, now occupied by new residents. The whole story is based on the couple's attempt to drive out the new homeowners who are alive, just the opposite of what we are used to watch, ghosts haunting homes and being driven out - in *Beetlejuice* the living that are the really scary. The production design and characters are usual of director Tim Burton and several of the elements will be re-written in films such as *The Nightmare Before Christmas* and *Corpse Bride*, always treating death and the macabre as something natural and even funny.

I could not fail to highlight the title character, Beetlejuice or Betelgeuse (Michael Keaton), the bio-exorcist ghost who wants to sell his services to the Maitland couple and expel the living inhabitants of the house. The film is successful in using Betelgeuse sparingly, with little time on the screen so we do not get sick of it but allowing he steal all the attention when he shows up. All the humor, especially when it has the Betelgeuse participation is cartoon style, using cartoon logic and physics and consequently very amusing.

Beetlejuice discards cohesion to create moments on the screen and this ends up meaning like writer laziness, since in this kind of movie, comedy with ghosts, any rule could be created and followed without problems because it is totally disconnected with reality. The whole second act - the middle of the film - seems unnecessary in terms of story and it does not have any sense, serving only to occupy space while awaiting completion. Regardless of the problems, *Beetlejuice* is unique in its own way and even if it is not a masterpiece it is still very much remembered even it is almost 30 years old.

Score: 3/5

They Wait (2007)

After the death of his uncle, Jason (Terry Chen), who used to live in Shanghai, goes to the United States for the funeral, accompanied by his family, the wife Sarah (Jaime King) and the son Sam (Regan Oey). Once in USA, stranger things begin to happen during the period of the Chinese Month of Dead, in this film that does not stand out for creativity but is efficient in its proposal.

They Wait utilizes the oriental spirits mythology, especially the Chinese, but their aesthetic is primarily western. The plot is interesting and catches the attention, with no easy scares (we do not have the old cat jumping out of the dark) and showing some surprising unfoldings. The strategy works to some extent because throughout the film the addiction to presenting excessive clues - small acts and expressions to reveal the true intents of certain characters - ends up spoiling some surprises. But the balance is positive and *They Wait* gives some frights and holds the attention with its good rhythm.

The horror genre is perhaps the one that most uses and overuses the clichés and even because of this and its popularity (which means many films of this type are produced) is one of the genres that most presents works of dubious quality. So when we see a movie that assumes it is a unpretentious entertainment, besides well done and interesting, there's nothing to complain about.

Score: 3/5

The Awakening (2011)

The year is 1921, England, home of Florence Cathcart (Rebecca Hall) whose job is unmasking ghosts and spiritist sessions, exposing the fraudulent and non-supernatural character of these events. She is called to unravel a ghostly apparition in a boarding school where reminiscences of her past will come back strongly enough to make Florence lose his mind and his emotional balance.

There are two interesting features, although not highlighted, in *The Awakening*: the backdrop surrounding World War I, which acted as a real ghost in British life and the chauvinism of early twentieth-century society, demonstrated by the fact that many characters being more frightened by the existence of a learned woman than by spirits. Discounting these factors, *The Awakening* is a generic horror film, using elements from dozens of other films such as *The Sixth Sense*, *The Others* and *Shutter*. The horror filmmakers' obsession with the astounding ending, which also happens in *The Awakening*, ends up destroying any logical succession of events within the plot, which is inflated with scares and attitudes that make no sense if seen with the final twist in mind. Another major problem is the heroine, Florence, whose confidence oscillates erratically, being much more passionate and irrational than would be expected for a ghost-hunter.

Even with positive points, such as the competent direction abusing of close-ups that in fact help to understand and tell the story and convincing performances, most notably the school housekeeper Maud (Imelda Staunton) and the boy Tom (Isaac Hempstead Wright), the balance is negative and *The Awakening* is not a good movie; may work as a simple entertainment, but leaves a bad taste if we dare to think rationally about its story after its completion.

Score: 2/5

Ghoul (2015)

Another film that, although not be exactly a found footage movie, has all the characteristics of this terror subgenre, with characters playing amateur cameramen who do not leave the camera even being stabbed or mutilated. Lazy and without any creativity, *Ghoul* even has a good premise , but it is annulled by the banality of this dispensable production.

Three young North American filmmakers go to Ukraine to shot a documentary about cannibalism. Supernatural events begin to happen, involving the spirit of Andrei Chikatilo, a real serial killer who was executed for his crimes in 1994 in Russia. The premise is good and involves a real criminal, which could give more depth to the story, but this is not what happens. The audience intelligence has been offended scene after scene, with the characters doing things in a unbelievable way, even for a story involving the supernatural. What we can do is hope with all our strength so that the unpleasant protagonists are soon killed by the spirit of Chikatilo.

Found footage subgenre has turned out a good crutch for less-talented filmmakers: the filming planning (découpage) is simpler, tension is easily created by the permanent subjective camera and any need for a logical plot is replaced by the need for a always shoting character. Near the movie conclusion, after unbelievable supernatural events, one character (holding a camera, of course) says to another, "What you're telling me does not make any sense". A film that brings that sentence at this point in the character development in a story of cannibal demons is what makes no sense at all.

Score: 1/5

Through the Shadow (2015)

Brazilian cinema does not have the tradition of performing supernatural thrillers and the closest it can get to this genre it is Coffin Joe movies in the 1960s and 1970s. *Through the Shadow* draws attention to the fact that it exploits this genre and delivers a reasonable result.

Teacher Laura (Virginia Cavendish) is hired to tutor a couple of siblings on a farm, but soon realizes that there is something strange about the place and the children. The revelations happen gradually, without big shocks and easy scares (cats running or loud sounds); on the other hand the pace starts slow, which is not a problem, but it does not follow the increase of the tension of Laura discovering the truth and this is a problem, because we are not able to feel the real impact of what is happening. This unique tone harms the film that, although well done and with good interpretations, does not provoke emotion what is terrible for a thriller.

Through the Shadow is simple and well produced and its plot, although far from being original, is well tied up and holds attention. Perhaps the over-cautiousness of the filmmakers so as not to fall into the traps of the horror genre has made the play too lukewarm.

Score: 3/5

American Poltergeist (2015)

American Poltergeist quickly sets the stage for his plot - some students rent a house to stay close to college and strange things begin to happen - leaving aside the development of the characters and because of that assuming the risk of the audience does not care about their destination. At first sight, the decision seemed correct, because it would allow the movie to gain pace and focus on the horror, but it was not long before I realized that the structure adopted was not the result of the planning done during the plot writing or the storyboard elaboration, but of the lack of talent of the filmmakers.

The characters depth is not the only problem of *American Poltergeist*: the story does not make sense, the actors seem to be doing school theater, the clichés are a constant and the worst, the film does not scare or create tension. In the movie we can note elements lazily and randomly blended from the main subgenres of terror like the supernatural, the psychological and in its final act the slasher (as *Friday the 13th*), when the spirit starts to chase the perverted young people (they were in a sex and drugs party) to execute them.

American Poltergeist passes the impression of being made by horror fans who wanted to use in their film everything they admired in other movies, lacking only to copy from their inspirational sources a minimum of quality.

Score: 1/5

The Boy (2016)

Why does looking at *The Boy* doll protagonist cause discomfort? This may be explained by a concept of robotics and is what prevents *The Boy* from being a complete disaster.

To escape an abusive relationship the American Greta (Lauren Cohan) takes up a job as a nanny in England. But the child Greta is going to take care of is a doll, handled by her parents like a real person because the trauma of the loss of her son Brahms (Jett Klyne) in a fire. Strange things begin to happen suggesting that the doll has a will of its own and is unbelievable the characters behavior, treating all those occurrences naturally and then quickly accepting the supposed supernatural character of the events. That alone would be enough to ruin the film, since it screams all the time to the audience: do not bother with these details, it's just a movie. But the filmmakers did not find this enough and created a twist in the conclusion that, although tie up some loose ends, is not convincing and takes much of the plot logic away. The good thing of the movie is the doll, which may not scare at all but it sure causes annoyance and I believe that this is due to the uncanny valley concept, that preaches that when a replicated artefact is very similar to a human being, but without being identical, this object causes repulsion to the watchers.

After all, the most scary thing about *The Boy* is Greta's boyfriend, Cole (Ben Robson), with his abusive and violent behavior. Taking itself too seriously while at the same time assumes its horror movie features, with its protagonists behaving exactly like film characters and not as minimally plausible people, *The Boy* benefited from a robotics hypothesis that eventually made him a movie, although far from good, at least bearable.

Score: 2/5

The Forest (2016)

It's very common in action movies that the writers, realizing that things are very quiet on the screen for many minutes, make up a scene whose sole aim is to create action, without much importance to the development of the story. There always these kind of scenes in movies, for instance, as the 007 agent franchise and is a forgivable expedient if used moderately. In *The Forest* that same idea is used for the scares and every couple of minutes something happens in an artificial way only to cause startles in the audience, highlighting the mediocrity of the movie.

Aokigahara is a forest in Japan actually used by suicides for its last ride and *The Forest* is based on that fact. Sara (Natalie Dormer) goes to Japan to find her twin sister Jess, missing and last seen in Aokigahara. The sad and interesting premise is wasted with silly scares and a loose story that can not at any time get the audience to empathize with Sara or Jess. Everything is crowned with a conclusion consistent with the rest of the film: an important character reappears as if by enchantment in the last minutes, there is an exaggerated massive ghost attack and the inevitable foolish and nonsense final scare before the credits.

The Forest misrepresents Aokigahara and the memory of those who died there, as the violence of the forest dwellers leaves in doubt the number of suicides and how many people were killed by the ghosts. And it raises another question: is it better to watch *The Forest* or to camp in Aokigahara? I'd rather the second option.

Score: 1/5

Haunted Minds (2016)

Haunted Minds is a Brazilian supernatural horror movie that despite the failures and the obvious inspiration in *The Sixth Sense* (1999), it captures the attention and manages to surprise with the secret revealed in its conclusion.

Davi (Bruno Garcia) is a psychologist who wrote a book where he demonstrates, through practical cases, that ghosts do not exist and are products of minds that have experienced some kind of trauma. I know this conclusion is obvious for any skeptical mind, but this kind of text can be useful for people raised involved by mystical traditions. The young Renata (Malu Rodrigues) asks for her help in trying to find out what happens to her sister Julia (Bianca Batista), who claims to be visited by the ghost of a former farm worker on the rural estate where she lives.

The production could be more subtle and leave the audience in doubt, at least for some time, about the supernatural nature of the events, but the ostensive and heavy soundtrack nearly shouts to the audience in the movie first minutes that a ghost will appear anytime. The psychologist David's behavior is also strange, for although he claims not to believe in ghosts and to say more than once that he is not a ghost hunter he acts as if he believed and as if he were looking for ghosts. This may even be explained by the true nature of his experiences, which will be revealed later, but the way he presents himself does not correspond to his acts.

Although production seems to need more resources - for example the farmhouse, clearly a poorly disguised hotel - *Haunted Minds* can deceive us and its surprising ending still makes sense even if we watch the film again aware of its twist and looking for flaws that compromise the logic of the solution - I did not find any errors. Far from being a masterpiece, *Haunted Minds* producers overcomes the obstacles of lack of money and delivers a decent movie.

Score: 3/5

The Bye Bye Man (2017)

Say his name, just think about his name and he will come.This is the premise of *The Bye Bye Man* and to speak, even if mentally, the name Bye Bye Man will invoke the entity that will not rest while the person who called him is not dead.

Even though it's not very original (there's no way I cannot remember *Candyman*), *The Bye Bye Man* keeps the interest by investing more in psychological horror than explicit one most of the time - the dreams with the train and the naked protagonists on the rails, as well as the coins that refer to the mythological ferryman Charon are good examples. The film avoids the easy scares and the director Stacy Title seems to joke around this, because there are several moments when the scare seemed to be imminent but it is avoided. In the last act, after the protagonist Elliot (Douglas Smith) understands the nature of the events he has experienced, *The Bye Bye Man* falls into the temptation to make the character an idiot, acting in the opposite way than he should and what he preached , all to facilitate the story conclusion.

The Bye Bye Man is not able to keep in its conclusion the good pace of its first half, speeding up and manipulating events probably in order to allow the inconclusive ending, which would allows sequels. Discounting this and the common absurdities in most of horror films - look out the size of the house in which the protagonists live, that seems to be much larger inside than on the outside, such as *The Evil Dead* hut - *The Bye Bye Man* is competent within your genre.

Score: 3/5

1922 (2017)

1922 is objective and frightening when telling the story of Wilfred James (Thomas Jane), who decides to kill his wife because of the woman's decision to divorce and sell her share of the family's estate. To make everything worse, he persuades his own son Henry (Dylan Schmid) to be an accomplice to the crime.

Everything happens quickly and by the end of the first act all the pieces are already positioned to the audience can witness Wilfred's downfall. From the moment the crime is committed the rats become a constant presence, representing both the rot in which the protagonist plunged as his feeling of guilt.

1922 is a fine example of a relatively simple but well-told plot, reaching its goal of showing real terror - danger can live in anybody's house and divide anybody's bed - even with elements that can be seen as supernatural (or not, since they could be only the result of James' imagination and guilt). Without being pretentious or wanting to prove to be more than it is and getting right to the point, *1922* is one of the best adaptations for the cinema of the Stephen King's work.

Score: 4/5

Vampires

Night of the Devils (1972)

The Italian movie *Night of the Devils* combines features of various horror films subgenres: trash, gore, psychological terror and even some eroticism. The result, although irregular, is a movie that avoids the vices and clichés of vampire films.

Nicola (Gianni Garko) is on business travel in Italy when, due to an accident with his car, he need to ask for help to a family living in the middle of a forest. All this events are shown in flashback, while Nicola is hospitalized, a trick that greatly helps to catch the audience attention. There is something wrong about the family and the movie improves as the suspense over what is actually happening is maintained. When the vampire curse is revealed, *Night of the Devils* avoids stereotypes like crosses, melting bodies under sunlight and even thirst for blood - here the vampires just attack to create similar ones. On the other hand, the low production budget is evident, even with the talent of the great Carlo Rambaldi as special effects master. The excessive exposure of viscera and destroyed faces could have been avoided, making the film less appealing and exposing much less the lack of resources.

Even with its excesses, *Night of the Devils* is a good movie that uses the ancient mythology of the vampires in a different way to which we are accustomed. If we ignore the amount of red-tinted corn syrup, we can enjoy this story of vampires who only seek other beings to share their eternal existence.

Score: 3/5

Near Dark (1987)

Creatures without charm or sophistication, more like a bunch of troublemakers living on the streets at the cost of petty thefts and murders to quench the hunger for blood. These are the vampires from *Near Dark*, film which starts in a promising way by showing the blood drinkers as monsters without glamour, but surrenders to the clichés and ends up turning into a sugary love story.

Caleb (Adrian Pasdar) flirts with female vampire Mae (Jenny Wright) who ends up biting and turning the young man in love into a bloodthirsty monster. The boy then joins the girl and her group in order to learn how to live as a vampire. The good ideas of the movie, like its first scene showing in detail a mosquito sucking blood from a human arm, soon run out and the plot suffers to fill the 90 minutes of the projection, since its plot is simple and without big twists. The production gives the impression of a bad development, where there was a good initial idea but little content to expand it; soon the easy solutions begin to be shown on the screen, with unbelievable coincidences and improbable attitudes of both the villains and the victims, all in the service of a lazy script.

Disappointment is the best word to define *Near Dark*, since its beginning seemed to indicate that it would be at least a reasonable movie. The conclusion, childishly and artificially happy, not only confirms its lack of quality but also reinforces its mediocrity.

Score: 2/5

Cronos (1993)

Cronos is a story of vampires with the differential of not treating the phenomenon as supernatural, but as a result of the human intellect. In the movie the cronos device is used to obtain eternal life and vampirism is nothing more than the set of side effects of treatment, such as need for human blood and extreme light sensitivity.

Cronos is the first feature film by director Guillermo del Toro and we can already observe his care with the details and production design - for example is notable how the cronos machine is creative and well executed. On the other hand, there are silly and underutilized symbologies, as the protagonist who is called Jesus and the fact that he resurrected (even more it's Christmas time).

With its qualities and small deficiencies, *Cronos* renews the figure of the vampire disassociating it of the supernatural explanations and incorporating it to the modern society; as a result it prepares the audience for new vampire mithology elements like *Blade*'s technology and *True Blood*'s artificial blood.

Score: 3/5

From Dusk Till Dawn (1996)

From Dusk Till Dawn is actually two movies inside one: the outstanding first half, with increasing violence and tension and the second half, where the supernatural takes over the plot and the movie becomes a trash horror film.

The change of tone between the two segments is so glaring that it's as if we're watching another movie with the same characters. It is not just a thematic change, but also a total transformations in the rhythm and in the approach. The realistic terror of the beginning, with the criminal brothers Seth (George Clooney) and Richard Gecko (Quentin Tarantino) demonstrating in each scene how dangerous they are, does not allow the audience to breathe and we always try to anticipate what the two bad guys will do next. In its second half, the supernatural terror takes over, the gore is the strongest feature and little happens, torturing the audience with a long, loose and meaningless sequence. To make matters worse, everything is very badly done and there are scenes where the heroes (or anti-heroes) talk surrounded by the monsters and the the monsters wait the end of dialog to strike again.

From Dusk Till Dawn tried to innovate by mixing seemingly incompatible elements but the film did not work not for this reason but for failing to maintain the cohesion in several dimensions like theme, rhythm and tone, besides wasting characters and great situations, like the sexual tension between Richard Gecko and Kate (Juliette Lewis) and the loss of faith of Pastor Jacob (Harvey Keitel) - in the conclusion the recovery of Jacob's faith only served him to convert common water into holy water. *From Dusk Till Dawn*, even with all the talented names involved in its production, achieves the feat of making people sleep to the sound of vampires being shattered.

Score: 3/5

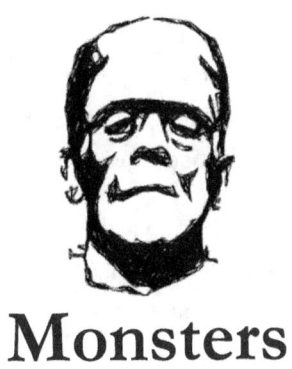

Monsters

Frankenstein (1931)

The figure of the *Frankenstein* monster is iconic - though it is not really plausible, what the meaning of apparent bolts in a corpse? - and much of Earth's population knows what it is about seeing images of actor Boris Karloff made-up as the creature. Even though the weak and sometimes foolish plot, *Frankenstein* is a classic for its images and cinematographic techniques and the film is still convincing today, almost 90 years after his debut.

In the opening scene, Edward Van Sloan appears on the screen in front of a curtain, warning the audience of what they were about to witness and advising the weakest to give up while it was time. This marketing strategy may even seem a bit dishonest but it worked, making everyone concerned and anxious to see the movie. Soon, several scenes that have been present in the imaginary of the twentieth century people begin to emerge: the scientist Henry Frankenstein (Colin Clive) and his humpback assistant Fritz (Dwight Frye), the bed with the monster being raised to receive the rays that will give him life again, Henry shouting "It's alive, it's alive!", the creature coming through the window in Henry's bride's room Elizabeth (Mae Clarke) and finally the burning mill in the ending. The simple structure based on images -

there is not even soundtrack punctuating the scenes - stablish the film in the audiences's mind almost shot by shot, demonstrating *Frankenstein* strength. There are problems like the second act, which shows how the monster rebels after being resurrected, which is too fast and unconvincing and Colin Clive as Henry Frankenstein, grotesque and overacting, almost laughable, appearing to be acting in a silent movie.

Regardless of the defects, *Frankenstein*'s scenes remain striking, even though it is not a brilliant film and not even on the list of the greatest terror movies - 1922's Nosferatu, for example, is better - but the sense of déjà vu we have seeing Frankenstein - at the premiere time people must have had the feeling of jamais vu - it demonstrates the movie geniality.

Score: 4/5

Wer (2013)

Wer brings the lycanthropy to the real world and explains the curse as a disease, the porphyria. The basic storyline sounds like a good idea if well developed but *Wer* fails to turn this plot into a good movie, delivering a meaningless film and with all the vices and clichés of the horror genre.

The only good thing about *Wer* is the competent makeup, extremely realistic and well done. Putting the makeup aside, we can find the false scares with animals (usually cats are used but here the poor victims are pigs and bats), the traditional police incompetence and the total irrationality of heroes in dealing with mortal danger. In some scenes it is hard not to laugh so absurd is the situation that is happening on the screen. And if on the one hand the film tries to show the werewolf not as a monster but as a sick person, on the other hand it is impossible to attribute to any non-supernatural being the resistance and strength demonstrated by the creature.

Wer causes real dread in the audience at its stupid conclusion, that has problems of continuity and it is not able to show the slightest logic. Further, the ending opens the possibility for sequels: spooky!

Score: 2/5

The Shallows (2016)

The man (or rather, the woman) against nature, a recurring theme in the cinema since its inception and sharks, natural born villains loved by Hollywood - *Sharknado* and its countless sequels illustrate this observation. This said, *The Shallows* is another shark film but simple, well done and honest in its intentions.

Nancy (Blake Lively) is surfing on a secluded beach in Mexico on the pretext of being alone after losing her mother to cancer. The mother story is used to give a pretentious depth to the film and amplify the emotional moments, but it is obviously in the background because in a movie like that what matters is the shark and the danger faced by the heroine, creating good moments of tension. It's remarkable that the situations created are plausible - let's forget about the shark's unusual intelligence and obsession - and it's easy to believe what we're seeing. Nancy is in an environment that is not hers, all nature seems to plot against her and we can feel the pain and the affliction caused by the situation.

The Shallows is not pretentious and shows correct decisions at various points, like its rhythm, its duration, its situations and of course, in the shark. Even yielding to cheap sentimentality in one or two scenes, it embraces the cinema fun without fear and worth to be seen, even if it is forgotten shortly after we leave the theater.

Score: 3/5

Antibirth (2016)

Usually I try to be optimistic about the quality of the movie I'm watching, trying to find out positive aspects from the artistic point of view and non-obvious meanings. It's hard to maintain that intent with *Antibirth*, and it's virtually impossible to find interesting qualities or signs in this movie.

Lou (Natasha Lyonne) is addict in the most diverse types of licit and illicit drugs and she discovers that is pregnant after attending a party where she is certain she has not had sex. How the plot could be developed from then on? As a modern version of the Christian mythology of Mary, invoking Godard in *Je vous salue, Marie*? Or maybe with a message warning of the danger of drug use in pregnancy? None of this, everything develops like a mixture of terror and science fiction without rhythm, without sense, without suspense, without horror.

Everything gets even worse in the conclusion - attention, spoiler ahead - which shows Lou giving birth to a monstrous head (?!) - yes, only the head, the body comes next, what causes the literal emptying of Lou's body.

If you ignored the spoiler alert and figured out how *Antibirth* ends, worthy of the horror movies made for home video in the 1980s, you might avoid watching *Antibirth*. In this case you will miss out just one thing: finding out how you would feel in a bad trip.

Score: 1/5

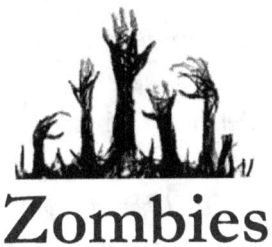

Zombies

Night of the Living Dead
(1968)

The zombie mythology in the cinema, as we know it nowadays, is totally based on *Night of the Living Dead*, directed by George Romero with modest resources and full of good ideas.

All of the elements that sound like ordinary today - slow zombies that can infect through the bite and be killed with a head shot - were already in this 1968 film and even if it is debatable whether they were created or copied, the fact is that they were formatted and compiled in *Night of the Living Dead*. Looking carefully, most if not all contemporary zombie movies are somehow remakes from *Night of the Living Dead*. Even the central idea of TV show The Walking Dead, the conflicts between humans and their behavior in an extreme situation, had already been explored by Romero in his film showing that humans, largely because of their unpredictability, are more dangerous than zombies.

With few frights and relatively soft violence for a film of this genre, *Night of the Living Dead* stands out for its atmosphere, ambiance and plot, never falling into the temptation of unbelievable behaviors or improbable solutions. It's a dry and realistic movie on the hypothesis that the zombies are real and that makes it so scary.

Score: 4/5

Contracted (2013)

It is difficult to define *Contracted*: is it a supernatural horror, is it a movie about an epidemic, is it a drama or a zombie movie? The difficulty in fit it in a genre, which can be a compliment for some films, here only demonstrates how lost are the *Contracted* producers.

Samantha (Najarra Townsend) is facing difficulties in her relationship with Nikki (Katie Stegeman) and ends up being raped at a party. From there, she begins to develop a strange sexually transmitted disease and her life begins to crumble. There is an interesting sign, associating the flowers - sexual organs of vegetables - with Samantha's health. But there is not much left over: the casting is wrong and everyone seems too old for their personalities and attitudes, there are stereotypes and symbols so explicit that they even become embarrassing, like the tattoo in Nikki's hand with the word rebel or the scene in which Samantha's conservative mother appears framed "fitted in" under a cross. It is also worth mentioning the implicit moralism, which tells that the girls who do not behave will end up giving themselves harm.

I do not know if *Contracted* wanted to make a parallel with AIDS or the devastation caused by the consumption of some drugs, such as crack. Whatever the intention, the goal has not been achieved and *Contracted* does not work as a medium for any message or even just for fun.

Score: 2/5

Maggie (2015)

Utilizing the widely known zombie mythology, *Maggie* avoids commonplace and tells an intimate story, chronicling the last days of infected Maggie (Abigail Breslin) next to her father (Arnold Schwarzenegger) before she turns into a zombie.

The tone is already noticeable by the title - *Maggie* - that avoids terms related to terror or action and privileges the character. The metaphor with real terminal illnesses and the hypocrisy of people facing death are clear: life itself does not belong to the person, who is condemned to die as society wants, no matter how much suffering it represents, as if everyone were forced to pay the sins imposed by Judaeo-Christian beliefs.

Perhaps because of its discreet tone and its somewhat generic artistic elements - music and cinematography mainly - *Maggie* was little seen and commented. It deserved more recognition, after all it is one of the few films of our beloved undead focusing a more serious and adult theme.

Score: 3/5

Train to Busan (2016)

Zombies who run after their victims instead of crawling and whose bodies are not blown apart by a single blow. Besides that, they walk in hordes of hundreds, huddled like insects. I'm not talking about *World War Z* but a much better movie, the Korean film *Train to Busan*, which handles zombie mythology in a different, raw and dynamic way.

Following the disaster movies formula, some characters are introduced to accompany them on a train trip between the South Korean cities Seoul and Busan. The format does not bring news but everything has a near-perfect presentation and development. The scenes accurately convey all the chaos caused by the infection, causing tension and distress even though it is relatively easy to imagine which characters will not die - at least to some extent in the story.

Some plot points resemble *The Walking Dead* by showing that humans are as dangerous or even more dangerous than zombies, but in general the harm comes from the infected ones, always hunting in large numbers and being extremely fast. These characteristics of *Train to Busan* zombies allow the creation of memorable sequences such as the first stop of the train in an infested station and the monsters chasing the train by creating a bridge with their bodies in the same way some species of ants do in the real world.

There is no subject that does not allow a new and well made approach, even a subject as exploited as the zombies and *Train to Busan* is a proof of this. The attention to details, great execution and the courage to produce a zombie movie without wanting to impose a supposed artificial depth, all this makes Zombie Invasion a great movie.

Score: 4/5

Get Out (2017)

Using the horror movie format, *Get Out* deals with the way racism is rooted in small acts, as well as showing other modes of prejudice through racial stereotypes - the athletic black guy, the sex machine black guy. Keeping the tension atmosphere all the time, only sins in small details that could have been easily avoided.

Chris (Daniel Kaluuya) dates Rose (Allison Williams) and goes to the girl's parents house to meet them. The white family conveys the idea of liberality, progressiveness and tolerance but Chris soon realizes that everything sounds artificial and something is wrong. It is remarkable how tension is present at all times and the feeling that Chris is in great danger is palpable.

It is impossible to express or simulate what a victim of prejudice feels like, but the film somehow emulates the feeling and at various moments we feel the discomfort and fear of Chris. Nonviolent prejudice, those eyes following the victim, like a black boy being watched by security guards at a fancy store, is shown efficiently but not only that. The other, which many consider erroneously as a compliment, the stereotype that makes the individual one-dimensional: the black athlete, who is supposed to have genetics in his favor and must take advantage of this, the black stallion, which must satisfy every woman who appears in from of him. This diminishes the person because it does not give him the choice of being what he wants, such as hating sports or being romantic for example.

Behind these remarkable signs, we have an extremely efficient movie in keeping us glued to the chair. The final part loses its strength a little, both by the end of the mysteries and by some simplistic and illogical solutions to reach the conclusion, such as the enlightening photos found by a character almost by miracle or the way the same character get rid of captivity having his hands immobilized. More than simplistic, this type of artifice ends up destroying the immersion and reminds us that all this is just a movie. But in the end, even if imperfect, *Get Out* achieves the feat of being an effective horror film with social depth, rare case in this genre.

Score: 4/5

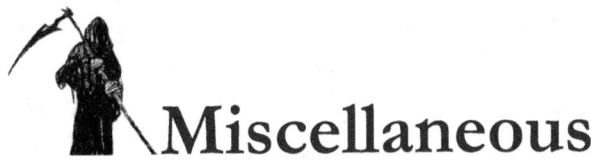

Destiny (1921)

Fritz Lang's *Destiny* is a example of the rich German expressionist cinema, a permanent influence on movie art and often cited as one of Alfred Hitchcock's favorite films.

After losing her groom, a young woman (Lil Dagover) meets Death (Bernhard Goetzke) to beg for the return of the beloved. Tired of its work, Death tells the woman three tales, each one taking place at different age and location but similar to young woman story, exposing that love is not enough to prevent the Reaper from performing its mission. Besides the universal appeal plot, *Destiny* offers us a unique ghostly atmosphere and purposely caricatured characters - which ends up bringing to some comic relief to the film - that enhance mythic nature of the movie. The attention to detail is another highlight and nothing of what we see on screen is unnecessary or superfluous, rewarding the most attentive viewers as in the case of the baby who appears briefly in the hands of death and suddenly fade - only near the conclusion it is explained that baby almost died during childbirth but survived.

Seminal film not only in narrative and artistic work - filmmaker Luis Buñuel said that after watching *Destiny* he discovered what he wanted out of life: making movies! - but also in the visual effects - the actor Douglas Fairbanks bought the film rights in the United States but delayed the release in order to reproduce the special effects for the movie starring himself, *The Thief of Bagdad* - *Destiny* also has a final bittersweet message: love only conquers death by surrendering to it.

Score: 5/5

Cat People (1942)

Cat People is a lesson in how to make a great feature film with a low budget, using creativity and cinematic techniques to suggest much more than showing.

Irena (Simone Simon) is an immigrant living in the United States who marries Oliver (Kent Smith). The marriage is not going well: the girl does not allow her husband touch her body, because she fears that when having sex with Oliver, she could turn into a panther and kill him, because of an ancient curse of his native land, Serbia. There are some scenes with panthers, mostly caged in a zoo, but most of the tension is created by the shadows, noises and a lot of suggestion.

The curse can be interpreted as a metaphor for the female repression that makes the women feel fear of sexual pleasure. Female pleasure was something to be avoided, for it would be unnatural and sinful, turning women into irrational beasts. There is an excerpt from the plot that corroborates this hypothesis: the panthers attendant on the zoo talks to Irena that the cats are demonic, as quoted in the Bible describing the Beast (in the biblical mythology) as a panther.

Cat People had a remake in 1982 that could not achieve the same quality of the original movie, a dry and straight to the point film, whose duration of only 73 minutes is enough to develop, tell and conclude the story.

Score: 4/5

Pit and the Pendulum (1961)

Roger Corman's *Pit and the Pendulum* is a simple and honest adaptation of Edgar Allan Poe story. This film is one of several adaptations from Poe's tales produced by director Corman, known as the master of the B movie.

The production is more sophisticated than most Corman films, with well-constructed scenarios and a convincing castle both from inside, with its detailed torture chamber, as from outside, when it can be seen all along the road. The production design is necessary to live up to the plot created by Poe, macabre and much more focused in the characters psychology than in the supernatural powers.

The story invites us to discover the circumstances that led to the death of Elizabeth Barnard (Barbara Steele), wife of Nicholas Medina (Vincent Price). Nicholas, son of a cruel and already deceased Spanish inquisitor, is psychologically fragile because of the bloody history of his family.

The atmosphere of the film is able to reproduce the discomfort caused by the text of Poe, transmitting the hardness of living in a castle haunted not by ghosts but by the echoes of the suffering and pain of those who perished there. The star Vincent Price has an ambiguous performance, playing like a monster (in a positive way) at times and grotesque in others, especially when trying to demonstrate the vulnerability of Nicholas.

The fragilities of *Pit and the Pendulum* - the simplification of the original text and the somewhat caricatured mise-en-scène - do not compromise the film amusement or prevent it from being an adaptation that respects its source of inspiration.

Score: 3/5

The Nightmare Before Christmas (1993)

Jack Skellington (voice of Chris Sarandon when speaking, voice of Danny Elfman when singing) is a skull and the King of Halloween Town, responsible for leading the monsters and organizing Halloween but he is tired of doing the same thing, although brilliantly, year after year, presenting the typical symptoms of the midlife crisis. He then discovers Christmas Town, amidst several doors leading to different cities representing the American holidays (among them Valentine's Day, Easter, Saint Patrick's Day) and decides to rule, in addition to Halloween, Christmas too. This plot that seems to be the result of a feverish delirium has turned into a stop motion animation whose great highlight is its fantastic look and their original characters.

The images from the frames of *The Nightmare Before Christmas* are unforgettable and have already become anthological in the cinema. The story is simple, but thanks to its relatively short duration (only 76 minutes) and the dynamic editing, the rhythm remains constant, all the time showing interesting things happening and leading the plot forward. The songs composed by Danny Elfman, a traditional partner of

Tim Burton (contrary to the common sense Burton is not the director of this film but the writer and creator of the characters - the director is Henry Selick), are not fabulous but are competent enough so that we are humming the musical themes when we leave the cinema.

The strength of *The Nightmare Before Christmas* is mainly its art design, but we must not forget its beautiful and fluid animation and that should be even more valued when we remember the immense effort of producing animation frame by frame, by stop motion technique. Regardless of its story, which may be considered foolish or too American, it is a film to be admired for its artistic beauty, which compensates for any deficiencies that may be observed.

Score: 4/5

Population 436 (2006)

The census officer Steve Kady (Jeremy Sisto) goes to the small town of Rockwell Falls to check the civil records to find out why the local population remains precisely stable - 436 people - for several decades. At first sight the story can sounds promising but the development creates a weak film and with a conclusion that makes everything worse.

The plot of the stranger coming into a closed society is not new and it has already been taken to the screen in good films, such as 1973 *The Wicker Man*, starring Christopher Lee. *Population 436* renews the idea in a thought-provoking way, adding the mystery of the stable population: why 436 people, how does this hold for so many years? After the initial curiosity the plot falls into the commonplace, with people sneaking up behind others just to deliver an easy scare and the spooky appearance of the residents, screaming to the audience with their intimidating glances, that the hero Steve Kady is in danger and should never have appeared by over there. Although ordinary, the development of the story keeps the interest until we get close to the conclusion, where things happen so fast we have the feeling that many days have passed but it was only one night. Finally we reach the mediocre ending, that suggests a supernatural force that so far seemed to be only inside the head of the fanatic citizens.

The writers of *Population 436* fell into the trap they had prepared themselves, not knowing how to untie the knot created by fantastic events made to catch the eye of the audience, forcing them to appeal to supernatural power. What could be a good entertainment has become a movie to be avoided.

Score: 2/5

The Cabin in the Woods (2012)

Caricatural characters, unlikely behaviors, clichés of all kinds: this is the tonic of most horror films. *The Cabin in the Woods* embraces these commonplaces but tries to explain them from a logical perspective within its fantastic diegesis.

Five friends travel to an isolated hut in the woods to have fun, that means having sex and smoking marijuana. This basic plot is almost mandatory in slasher horror films - adding a psychopathic murderer killing randomly - and the murders are seen almost as a punishment for young "sinners." The difference in *The Cabin in the Woods* is that behind these well-known elements there is an organization manipulating everything, from the roles assumed by the young - the macho man, the coy girl, the silly guy - to unbelievable attitudes such as entering an unknown basement and invoking spirits. I will not reveal here the agenda of those behind the events in the hut so as not to spoil the surprise of those who have not yet seen the movie, but everything fits well into the universe that the film represents, even if there is the supernatural element that allows any kind of horror to be embedded within the mechanics of the plot.

The Cabin repeats tired horror formulas in an innovative way, making the audience watch something familiar and new at the same time. In cinema the ideas are and will always be repeated and copied and what really matters is the way this is done. To top it all off, the *The Cabin in the Woods* filmmakers were brave enough to deliver a conclusion that does not support sequels - at least not a obvious one - even though they created a structure that would allow several other films. Because of the good movie box office, I think it will be difficult the producers not to be pressured to make more, even if it is not a sequel but a prequel. If it is well done as the original will be a pleasure to watch.

Score: 3/5

Regression (2015)

Regression is a psychological horror movie that does not give in to the temptation to seek easy supernatural explanations, but it induces the audience to believe in the extraordinary by not so fair ways.

Angela Gray (Emma Watson) accuses her father of committing physical abuse and the police has been called. From then on, a complicated plot unfolds, involving a supposed satanic sect consisting of several members of the small community. While the film succeeds in maintaining interest and suspense most of the time, it errs by deceiving the public too much with hallucinations that lead to the conclusion that there is the action of fantastic entities. It is plausible to accept the mental disturbance of Angela's relatives but the manipulation is evident when the disturbances take the policeman Bruce (Ethan Hawke). In the end it is explained - and it is a scientific truth - that regressions, even when done by professional psychologists, can create false memories in patients, but what happens to Bruce, who does not go through any regression session during the entire story, is clearly made just to create fake clues and increase the duration of the movie.

Regression begins very well and ends up losing itself in its eagerness to surprise. If we look carefully, *Regression* begins to fall apart after the scene using the cat's scare cliché - if a contemporary movie still uses this feature is because the ideas are exhausted.

Score: 3/5

Death Note (2017)

Based on the manga Desunōto from the early 2000s and already adapted both in animations and live action movies, *Death Note* is relatively true to its source, which is good in some ways but helps ruin the movie in others.

The story is fascinating: student Light Turner (Nat Wolff) finds a notebook - the death note - that gives his or her owner the power to kill anyone he or she wants, anywhere in the world, just by writing the name of the target on notebook while mentally visualizing the victim's face. A good plot decision - thanks for fidelity to the original material - is do not restrict Turner killings to personal revenge. Turner decides "clean up" the world by eliminating all criminals, assuming the identity of Kira, an avenging god who wants to reestablish justice. The film lacks, however, a certain seriousness that would give more weight to the whole plot. Part of the fault of this is, in addition to visual identity and editing both similar to a videoclip, the use of elements of the manga that do not work on the screen, such as Detective L (Lakeith Stanfield), who never convinces of his supposed genius, looking like a spoiled rapper. The excess of coincidences, perhaps due to the need to condense many events that probably took months in just 90 minutes, also bothers and it is hard to believe in the plausibility of just Tuner's father leading the investigation into the deaths caused by Kira. Everything worsens in the last act when the notebook, which originally served only to name who would be killed, becomes almost a computer terminal where people can be coded, with complex orders and conditional structures. As the icing on the cake, we can watch, near the conclusion, a chase scene that can be used as a cliché catalogue of this type of sequence: all tricks are used, from sliding cars in the street (incredibly through a kitchen!!) to finishing in a dead end.

Death Note as concept is a great idea and perhaps could work better as a TV series, perhaps showing the notebook with several owners at different time ages, not to mention the shinigami (demon) Ryuk (voice of Willem Dafoe) whose look is both fascinating and spooky. But the end result is, perhaps due to excessive reverence for the original material, perhaps because of the laziness or even lack of talent of the producers, disappointing.

Score: 2/5

Mother! (2017)

Some people may not like Darren Aronofsky's movies but it's impossible being indifferent to them. *Mother!* is no exception and watching it is an intense, visceral, even sometimes unpleasant experience. While we are watching *Mother!* there are moments that we hate it, but when the movie ends the more you think about *Mother!* the more you admire it.

The Aronofsky direction is so competent that all the discomfort felt by Mother (Jennifer Lawrence) is shared by the audience, in suffocating scenes with claustrophobic close-ups, intensifying the feeling of anguish. The story of the couple who has their quiet life tormented by strangers and more and more unwanted guests is just an allegory of something much bigger and to talk about it is necessary to reveal spoilers and interpret the movie in a way that can spoil the experience of those who have not yet seen it, so if you have not yet seen *Mother!* do not read the text beginning in the next page.

Mother! it's not a conventional horror movie , though some features may lead to this conclusion, such as the seemingly haunted house and events that do not appear to be natural. Actually *Mother!* is a fable about divine creation and destruction, according to the Christian-Catholic point of view. The character Him (Javier Bardem), the husband of Mother, is actually God as seen in the Bible and Mother is the incarnation of the feminine, that can be seen as Mother Nature, as the Virgin Mary or even as the representation of oppressed women by the Judeo-Christian patriarchal culture. The God depicted in the film is vain and oblivious, caring about only for worship and admiration for his work. Mother is maintainer, totally absent from vanity, wanting to just keep her home - the nature, the planet, the universe - intact and free from the destruction caused by the most beloved work of Him, the men. Several biblical characters parade on the screen, such as Man (Ed Harris) who would be Adam and his wife Woman (Michelle Pfeiffer) who would be Eve, as well as their children who end up fighting as in the biblical episode of Cain and Abel. There is also the baby (Jesus) who is killed after being offered by his father to the horde of devotees in a scene that is already among the most shocking in film history.

There are other layers and signs in *Mother!* and we can see how women are seen and treated - thanks to the talent of the director we feel in the skin of Mother -

and the folly and fanaticism of men. The film also unites, in a way, science and religion by showing the couple's home to be destroyed and recreated by Him in an infinite cycle that can be translated as the Big Bang, the explosion that gave rise to the universe and the Big Crunch, one of the hypotheses about the end of the universe that would be a great contraction bringing together all matter at one point and restarting the cycle.

The discomfort and reflexions caused by *Mother!* are typical of great masterpieces, whose purpose is not only to delight the audience but to cause discomfort, to provoke new ideas, to connect concepts and maybe to change the mental model of those who appreciate it.

Score: 5/5

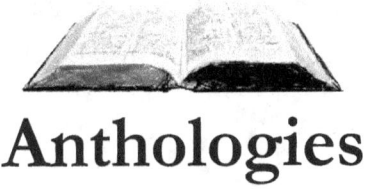

Anthologies

Spirits of the Dead (1968)

It seemed like a good idea, three stories by Edgar Allan Poe adapted by great directors, but the result is patchy:

Metzengerstein (Roger Vadim)
The plot strives to show Countess Metzengerstein (Jane Fonda) as cruel and libidinous, but fails in both attempts. It shows some beautiful moments, but most of the time it looks more like *Barbarella* in the middle ages.

William Wilson (Louis Malle)
The best of the three segments; tells the story of the doppelgänger (double) Wilson (Alain Delon) very well and maintains the tension all the time with the cruelties of the protagonist. It is the episode that best maintains the Poe's essence.

Toby Dammit (Federico Fellini)

This segment sounds as if someone is trying to imitate Fellini and not an authentique one, retaining a comic tone that completely alienates it from Edgar Allan Poe atmosphere. Neither Terence Stamp as the main character manages to save it.

Score: 2/5

Creepshow (1982)

An anthology of five horror stories presented as if they were drawn from a comic book called Creepshow - a tribute to the horror magazines of the 1950s. The film bears the face and charm of youth films of the 1980s, with great talents involved: directed by George Romero, written by Stephen King and makeup / special effects by Tom Savini.

All tales mantain the quality (they were all directed by Romero) and are as follows:

Father's Day
Daughter (not a child, an adult person) kills abusive father but he returns from the grave to take revenge. The plot demonstrates parricide is a unforgivable crime and the true evil never ends.

The Lonesome Death of Jordy Verrill
A meteor falls on Jordy Verrill's farm and his greed drives him to ruin. Funny and scary, still have as bonus Stephen King as a grotesque actor playing the protagonist.

Something to Tide You Over

The most frightening of the tales by being more realistic and with a more serious tone. After discovering his wife's cheating, psychopath Richard Vickers (Leslie Nielsen) performs a creative revenge against lovers, but his cruelty will not go unpunished.

The Crate

Could not be missing a monster movie in the anthology. An old box found in a university holds an ancestral evil so Professor Henry Northrup (Hal Holbrook) figure out a good use for the discovery. It bothers in the plot the fact that in a university, academics try to just get rid of the problem and not study it. But it develops the terror and suspense well and still shows a scary ending.

They're Creeping Up on You

Distressing for those who do not like insects, it shows how the vicious businessman Upson Pratt (E.G. Marshall) will be consumed by his own evil materialized as thousands of cockroaches. Impossible not scratching while watching, it is a segment only for who have a strong stomach.

Score: 3/5

3 A.M. 3D (2012)

Thai terror anthology with three stories that have in common the fact that the climax happens at 3 o'clock in the morning, supposedly the time when the ghosts would have their powers amplified. The result is not good in any of the segments:

The Wig

A ghost seeks revenge after the hair of her dead body were cut and sold to a wig shop. There is no new ideas, just the same old horror routines recycled mainly from other oriental horror films, the most of them from *Ju-on: The Grudge*. Its best scene turns out to be a dream, which even in a horror movie sounds like cheating.

Corpse Bride

A funeral home clerk needs to spend the night looking after two coffins (???) with newlyweds dead bodies who died in mysterious circumstances. The plot has some twists but the story does not make sense and, as in the previous segment, the best scene happens inside a dream. I do not need to say anything more.

O.T.

Two bosses are doing some horror pranks to their employees inside the company during the overtime period at early hours. Surprising at some times and without big plot problems, it still has the merit of hiding with competence the final twist. It is the best of the three segments, not that this is a great accomplishment.

Score: 2/5

Tales of Halloween (2015)

An anthology of horror with a characteristic that somehow highlights it from the others: instead of the three or four stories commonly showed in this type of movie here we have ten segments, all occurring during Halloween night, which works as isolated short films , although some characters appear in more than one of the segments - these crossovers have no relevance to the plots.

The nature of this type of film invariably produces an irregular quality and *Tales of Halloween* is no exception. There are some interesting episodes like **Trick**, where children deadly attack some adults inside a house with an astonishing conclusion and **The Night Billy Raised Hell**, with a macabre humor and curious development. The big problem is that everything was thought and done like a horror for the family, childish and too clean, not provoking scares and much less fear.

During some of the tales, in the television of the characters houses, is being broadcasted the 1968's movie *Night of the Living Dead*. More than a homage, this reference seemed to me like a filmmakers envy, because probably for commercial reasons they were forced to produce a horror movie for children.

Score: 2/5

+1 Horror Movie

The terror literature and

Perfume: The Story of a Murderer
(2006)

a murderer in search of
perfect perfume

by Rosângela D. Canassa, Ph.D.

The analysis of the movie *Perfume: The Story of a Murderer* seeks to find the motivations of the protagonist, who becomes a psychopath when he begins to manufacture perfumes. The psychological horror thriller was directed by Tom Tykwer.

The movie is based on Patrick Süskind's 1985 book, which sold more than 15 million copies worldwide and translated into 45 countries. Terror in literature has its origins in folklore and religious traditions, focusing on death, the idea of life after death, evil, demons and the beginning of something embodied to the person. These have manifested themselves in stories of witches, werewolves, ghosts and vampire species such as what happens in *Perfume: The Story of a Murderer*. The German Bernd Eichinger (*The Name of the Rose*) produced the film, which was shot in Germany, Spain and France in 2006, and reveals the atmosphere of eighteenth-century Paris in a faithful adaptation of the book.

Perfume tells the story of Jean-Baptiste Grenouille, born under a bench, where his mother used to sell fish, in a stinking redoubt in Paris in 1738. The fish, probably took from the River Seine, were already stinking and overlapping the smell of that place. Grenouille's mother had five deliveries right there in the fishmongery, cutting the umbilical cord with the same knife that cut her fish. The children were born dead, but Grenouille insisted on not accepting the same fate of his brothers and survived despite the attempt of infanticide on the part of the mother, who is executed by this.

The boy Jean-Baptiste began to speak only at the age of four, but barely communicated and then was raised in an orphanage and survived the aggressions of colleagues who repeatedly tried to smother him with the rags that covered his lean body. For little Grenouille, Madame Gaillard's establishment was a boon, but the woman was despicable, considering that children represented only money, selling them when necessary. The old lady nursed him until he was 13 years old, when Grenouille was sold to the local tanner.

In the Mr. Grimal's tannery Jean-Baptiste worked from dawn to dusk and he was a sweet and diligent boy, despite the poor working conditions. It was a childhood marked by child slave labor. Born in adverse circumstances, his life continued to be a matter of survival. He overcame various diseases and grew scarred, thin and ugly. But as a reward, still very young, he realized that he had a unique talent for discerning the odors around him, a fact that characterized his refined olfactory perception.

Walking through the streets of Paris, his nose took him to a beautiful, red-haired girl who wore a gray dress and sold nectarines. Grenouille walked toward him until he came close and smelled the intoxicating scent of the young woman. The scent was so soft and delicate that he could not retain it, fleeing her sense as she moved away from him.

He had the feeling that this scent would be the key to sort all the other scents and that he would not understand any scents if he had not fully understood it. He also realized that without possessing this aroma, his life would have no meaning, no grace. But he had to possess it and he could not. He felt a terrible fear of losing it forever.

When he came in contact with this scent, he was ecstatic and he knew that he had to capture that scent and that sublime beauty. The girl must was about thirteen or fourteen. When she realized there was someone sniffing her hair from behind, she was frightened and threatened to scream. Grenouille jumped up and covered his mouth. Unintentionally, in trying to keep her still, he killed the girl. That moment changed his life, impregnating his memories, his dreams, whether day or night.

After that, Mr. Grimal sells Grenouille to Giuseppe Baldini, an experienced Paris perfumer who realizes that the boy possesses an extraordinary sense of smell and begins to take care of him, teaching him the art of making oils, essences and fragrances. But, the boy soon overcomes his master in the manipulation of essences, when discovering new aromas, good or bad, it did not matter. He was not selective. His obsession became to discover all the odors of the world with the aid of Master Baldini. His unusual smell, which allowed him to distinguish and memorize scents with a singular ability to detect nuances in the odors, made him discover several aromas, thus enriching his Master.

As an apprentice at the perfume workshop, he became obsessed with finding out how to retain the scents and asked the perfumer to teach him. Jean-Baptiste begins to show his obsessive behavior in trying to know all sorts of odors and to retain them, when he kills Baldini's cat when trying to distill it, without success. He then departs for the city of Grasse, the world capital of perfumes, on the recommendation of Master Baldini to gain access to a technique of capturing the aroma and retain it.

But before reaching the city, he found a cave and there he had an almost mystical experience, in which he realized that his body had no odor at all. This made him realize that his existence depended on his own scent that did not exist, so he could even pass unnoticed through people because he did not have any smell. When he was a baby, the wet nurses complained that the child was strange, because he had no odor, and they did not want to be with him.

Grenouille unconsciously sought the scent of women, which could lead him to establish a connection with love in an unconscious way. Her thoughts and smell used to come involuntarily. He was afraid of not existing because he discovered that he was born deprived of any personal odor and, according to his criteria, devoid of identity. His quest for an essence symbolizes the pursuit of his own essence, the search for himself. Then his desire to capture the most sublime of all the scents which are subtracted from beautiful women is an attempt to steal from them the emanations and mainly retain the odor.

His obsession became deadly, by collecting human scents, turning him into a murderer of young and beautiful women. Excessive ambition and vanity are characteristic of psychopaths, such as serial killers. The search for strong sensations throughout his life evidences an attempt to feel his own body, compensating for the lack of feelings.

Another psychopath characteristic is the tendency to turn actions into impulses, often in an antisocial way and that does not provoke guilt or remorse. It all depends on the degree of psychopathy of the subject and homicide is the most extreme of his acting. He needs immediate satisfaction. He knows how to manipulate people to achieve his goals, and therefore many of them are successful, brilliant in their crimes, because they leave no trace, are implacable, endowed with intelligence, coldness and cruelty.

Jean-Baptiste Grenouille has this profile and he dresses a cloak that turns he into a fragile, poor man with no odor at all, that is, he passes through people without being noticed. In the town of Grasse, his goal was to become an exceptional being with the help of his nose and to manufacture the best perfume in the world, in a junction of odors taken from the women he pursued and killed.

In Grasse he began to work in a perfume factory and there learned to distil, through the enfleurage technique and met Laura, a young woman with red hair, freckles and green eyes, who reminded him of the young woman of Paris, who killed by accident. Creating his odor with frenezi, Grenouile needed to retain this sublime scent.

The fragrance of certain people, those extremely rare, who inspire love, these were their victims. He gave up taking custody of any living person and working with her and his new perfume. His goal was to steal the scent of certain women like Laura Richis. The young woman was hardly alone, for she had a father who would not leave her alone, for such beauty and fear of losing her, as he had lost his wife.

Antonie Richis had a single daughter at just 16 years old and her face was so beautiful that she received visitors of all ages and of both sexes, who were instantly paralyzed by such beauty. Even when his father looked at his own daughter, he looked upon her as a woman and cursed himself for his temptations that take peace from him.

In the Grenouille inner universe there is only the will to seize the world, the reality that surrounds it, through an illusion, creating a perfume capable of making everyone love him, through the twenty-fifth victim, the most precious, the most important for him, Laura Richis. She was the desire object of a murderer who wanted to receive love, but he was totally incapable of transmitting it and even of receiving it, as can be seen in the scene in which a bacchanal occurs in the middle of the public square in the light of day. Everyone there wants to hug him, kiss him, and he finally gets what he wanted: affection. But he only wishes to flee from there because he realized that he despised all mankind.

Laura's father was the deputy consul and worked with the manufacture of perfumes. He thought it was time to get a husband for his dear daughter and decided about choosing a husband. But the moment in the town of Grasse was troubled by several murders, girls found dead and naked, with shaven heads. Panic invaded the people who ran to protect their daughters.

Grenouille looked for the final ingredient to make up his ideal scent. A murderer in search of a perfect perfume. His ambition was not to enrich and to claim fame; he pursued the dream of dominating the hearts of men by creating a unique perfume, capable of arousing the deepest love in those who smell it.

A love dedicated to exclusively him, Grenouille, who only knew contempt and hatred. He knew he existed, but no odor, no mark, no identity, living in obscure lethargy, living as if he were a sleepwalker in the streets. The only desire he had within him was to discover the fragrance of love, of existence. He robs others of existence because he does not possess it. The scent of certain women he sought and whose odor and beauty he vampirized, trying to make up for what he lacked.

Since he never received affection, he lived encapsulated in himself and incapable of any kind of gift to the world. His communication was precarious, his expression poor, without a smile, a cry, a whisper. His real crime was his inability to love, to give himself, according to the author of the novel, Süskind.

Something happened to Grenouille: his smell, even though unconscious, turned into sexual attraction for the women he killed. It was not any woman he chose to seize his scent. His nose selected and hid secrets of attraction. Choices beyond your consciousness may be the result of projection games, that is, when you see in those who attract us our aspects or emotions from our past that are often re-edited.

Smell is the oldest sense of all, even bacteria can distinguish between nutritional and harmful substances by smelling their environment. Although the accuracy of human olfaction be ridiculous in contrast to other mammals, such as dogs and rodents. Even so, we have 347 types of sensory neurons in the olfactory epithelium. Each of them detects a different type of odor.

Our odors repertoire results from all possible combinations of these hundreds of receptors. Pheromones are involved in partner selection and sexual encounters in virtually the entire animal kingdom. Many species distinguish sex, social status, territory and reproductive status of the potential partner by the nose. In humans these processes are more complex, but there is evidence that people exchange secret and unconscious messages through pheromones. A discrete and delicate structure that connects the nose to the brain and that has gone unnoticed for centuries by scientists; the nerve Zero was originally identified in sharks and whales.

Thus, the Zero nerve and the unconscious reactions are the keys to understanding the unconscious choices of this character and the women by which he felt the intense attraction by his odor. Conscious desires are those that move freely in our psychic apparatus and do not present any difficulty to their location because they appear clearly, although when they appear in consciousness they may disturb. But unconscious desires are objects of repression, so it is more difficult to identify them. The object of desire, as well as most of the motivations for choosing a loving partner, is hardly clear to consciousness.

Sigmund Freud (1856-1939) emphasized in his studies that love relationships follow certain stereotypes that are repeated all the time, that is, we face past love experiences and then we transpose these experiences into the present, which constitute a situation in which past and present are mixed in a set of projections, we see ourselves in the one that attracts us, what is in us or that is part of our history (lived, fantasized or desired).

According to Freud, we love for a reason, to not getting sick and we get sick if we can not love. For Grenouille it was not possible to love nor be loved, so he fell ill with psychopathy.

As a consequence of Grenouille lack of affection, in addition to turn him into a psychopath also eventually created his fear of not existing. The search for a perfect perfumed essence, which is a metaphor for the search for himself, his essence, his soul. And according to the character Master Baldini: "THE SOUL OF BEINGS IS THEIR SCENT".

ABOUT THE AUTHOR

Fabio Consiglio studied film history and criticism with professors Inácio Araujo and Sérgio Alpendre, cinematographic language with Pablo Villaça and music in the cinema with Tony Berchmans.
He writes on Portuguese language blog faroartesepsicologia.blogspot.com and he is the author of the books Um Filme por Dia 2017 - Volumes 1 and 2.